FIGHTING FOR FREEDOM

ALONG THE UNDERGROUND RAILROAD

A HISTORY SEEKING ADVENTURE

by Shawn Pryor

CAPSTONE PRESS
a capstone imprint

Published by You Choose, an imprint of Capstone
1710 Roe Crest Drive, North Mankato, Minnesota 56003
capstonepub.com

Library of Congress Cataloging-in-Publication Data is available on the Library of
Congress website.

ISBN: 9781669032533 (hardcover)
ISBN: 9781669032717 (paperback)
ISBN: 9781669032625 (ebook PDF)

Summary: YOU are fighting for freedom from enslavement for yourself and others
during the mid-1800s. Will you escape to freedom? And will you help others
escape as part of the Underground Railroad's network of freedom fighters? Step
back in time to face the challenges and decisions that real people faced to escape
enslavement.

Editorial Credits
Editor: Mandy Robbins; Designer: Heidi Thompson; Media Researcher: Jo Miller;
Production Specialist: Tori Abraham

Image Credits
Alamy: North Wind Picture Archives, 24, 33, Science History Images, 91; Getty
Images: Bettmann, 10; Library of Congress, 16, 18, 36, 42, 46, 70, 93, 102, 105;
Shutterstock: Bigyy, 59, Colin Hui, 75, Eddie J. Rodriquez, 63, Everett Collection,
Cover, 50, 85, MakdIll, 81, Wolf Mountain Images, 57; XNR Productions, 4

All internet sites appearing in back matter were available and accurate when this
book was sent to press.

TABLE OF CONTENTS

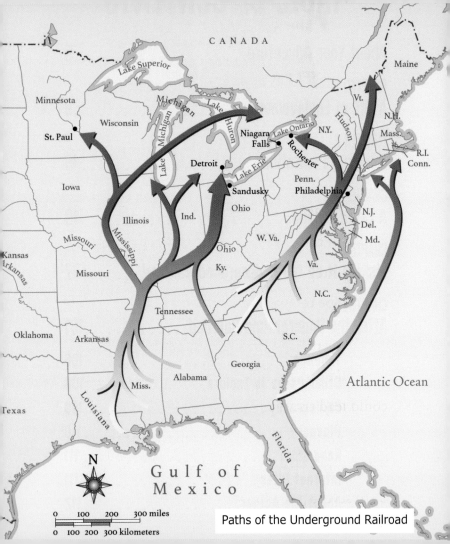

Paths of the Underground Railroad

ABOUT YOUR ADVENTURE

YOU are a Black person living in the United States in the mid-1800s. Most Black people in the country are enslaved. It's a hard life with very little hope of happiness or liberty.

If an enslaved person wanted to be free, they had to fight for it. The choices they made could lead them to freedom by escaping on the Underground Railroad or keep them enslaved. Every move they made might lead to a new life or to severe punishment or even death.

Now it's your turn to live through this difficult time in history. The events you'll experience could have happened to real people in the past. Chapter One starts the story. You choose which path to read. Follow the directions at the bottom of each page to continue your journey.

The choices you make will change your outcome for better or worse. After you finish your path, go back and try another path for a different perspective and even more adventures. YOU CHOOSE the path you take through history.

Turn the page to begin your adventure.

CHAPTER 1

A LIFE OF ENSLAVEMENT

The mid-1800s has been a time of exploration and expansion for the United States. Many people have prospered. But it has not benefited all Americans. Native people have had their homelands stolen from them. And a large portion of Black people are enslaved, mostly on large farms called plantations. They serve as forced labor camps in southern and Atlantic states.

Turn the page.

Black people on plantations are enslaved against their wills. Enslaved people are forced to work for large farming operations. Other enslaved people are servants for the owner—cleaning, cooking, and caring for their enslaver's children.

Enslaved workers in a cotton field

Enslaved people are heavily punished for any missteps. These punishments keep them fearful of their enslavers. Enslavers also have overseers who punish enslaved people. Punishment could be whipping, being chained in shackles, being beaten, hanged, imprisoned, or worse. The purpose of the punishment is to make sure that the enslaved know that their enslaver has power over them.

Enslaved people are usually denied access to education and personal activities. Enslavers keep the enslaved uneducated and working long hours to remove any form of joy from their lives. They sell parents and children away from the rest of their families. They want to make sure enslaved people feel helpless and dependent on them. They don't want enslaved people to know how to even try to escape.

Turn the page.

On rare occasions, an enslaver will free someone, usually upon the enslaver's death. But most enslaved people know that their only way to freedom is to escape. And their best shot at escaping is on the Underground Railroad. It is a network of routes, paths, and safe places for escapees. It is run by abolitionists in the United States. These people want to put an end to slavery. The Underground Railroad can take fleeing Black people to free states in America or as far as Canada.

You know that escaping enslavement has many dangers and finding the Underground Railroad can be difficult. Are you ready to fight for freedom?

- To escape from a forced labor farm with a group, turn to page 15.

- To ship yourself to freedom in a wooden crate, turn to page 49.

- To be a freed person working on the Underground Railroad, turn to page 77.

CHAPTER 2

FLEEING A PLANTATION

Life as an enslaved farm worker is exhausting and painful. You and your fellow workers sleep in a rickety barn on the farm. The cracks in the wooden slats let in a little breeze, but the August air is so muggy, it can't cool you down.

You struggle to sleep on your uncomfortable bunk made of hay. You recall when you were separated from your family years ago. You remember being sold to your current enslaver in Virginia.

Turn the page.

Homes for enslaved laborers

Suddenly, the barn door bursts open. A group of overseers splash buckets of water on everyone to wake you up. They leave a moldy loaf of bread for you to share.

One of the overseers yells, "Hurry up and eat your breakfast. If you're not out of this barn in five minutes, all of you will get the whip!"

The overseers leave as you all go for the bread and break it up evenly. You take a small bite of your bread and then take the rest of it over to your bunk. Behind your bunk of hay bales is a bag. You put your piece of bread in it. That should be just about enough food for your plan.

You are part of a group that tends the cotton and tobacco fields. This time of year, you pick the cotton, harvest the tobacco, and make sure that the fields are properly cared for. It is hard physical work. There are no machines to help you.

You're not even allowed a moment to rest in the heat. If you don't work fast enough or collapse from heat exhaustion, you're accused of laziness. The punishment is whipping. Luckily, the tobacco has grown more than six feet high in the fields. The tall plants can give you the cover you need to hatch your escape plan.

Turn the page.

Black people picking cotton by hand

Your calloused hands are scarred and
bleeding from picking cotton. But as you work,
you survey the land around you and keep mental
notes of your surroundings. Tomorrow night,
you will make your escape.

In the evening, after a long day of painful
work, all of you are in the barn huddled together.
You eat a meager dinner and tend to your
wounds, exhausted. You rub some mud on
your bloody fingers, listening to make sure the
overseers are gone.

"Okay, they're gone. It's just us," you say to the others.

"I can't keep doing this," said Jeremiah. "One of those overseers kept kicking me and telling me to work faster, but I was picking as fast as I could!"

Another man, Scott, was hunched over, as someone was tending to the lashes on his back. "He kept whipping me to see how long I could take it before I fought back. But if I tried to fight back, I knew it would get worse. I don't deserve this."

"None of us do," you say. You had planned to escape alone, but you realized you can't leave these people behind. "And I have an escape plan."

"What kind of plan?" asks Matilda. "You remember what happened when Jonas tried to escape? They killed him."

Turn the page.

You try to calm Matilda's fears. "He tried to escape during the day for everyone to see," you say. "If we leave in the middle of the night, there's less chance they will catch us."

"But where will we go?" Sylvester asked.

"I've heard of a safe house five miles north that is part of the Underground Railroad. The people there will hide us and sneak us away to the free states."

You go over to your bale of hay and get your bag to show the others.

"I've been storing food and supplies. The night watchman usually falls asleep in the middle of the night. And there should only be one or two guards in the fields. It's the best time to escape."

Xavier nervously asks, "But what if we get caught?"

"What's the difference?" you respond. "If we stay here, we'll be worked to death. I'd rather die trying to get free! I'm leaving tomorrow night. You all can come with me or stay here."

The next night, you and several others are ready to escape. All is quiet as you wait to hear the night watchman's snores. When you think you hear them, you signal the others. "Let's go," you whisper.

You walk across the farm, quietly. Any noise from you or your companions could mean disaster. After a few minutes, you've made it to the tall tobacco fields.

As you walk into the tobacco fields, the plan is going perfectly. The tobacco plants hide you well. In a while, you'll be near the woods and off the farm for good.

Turn the page.

Suddenly, you trip over a rock in the field and catch yourself on the ground.

"Hey, did you all hear that?" you hear one guard ask another.

"Eh, it's probably just the wind," says the other man.

You signal for everyone to be still and quiet.

"I heard ruffling over yonder. Let's check it out! Bring the dogs!" the first guard responds.

• To split up and go on your own, go to the next page.
• To stay together and not move, turn to page 25.

You've got to split up to confuse the guards. They can't catch all of you.

You motion to everyone to split up. You and your group go your separate ways. You run as fast as you can! The dogs bark as they ruffle through the fields toward you. Faster and faster, they come!

"Someone's trying to escape! Over there!" a guard screams.

"No, it's coming from over there!" says another guard.

"They're all over the tobacco field! Round them up before they make it to the woods! Hurry!" says an overseer.

Tobacco plants slap you as you run for your life. If you get caught, your punishment will be severe. You may even be killed. The guards are getting close, but you know you're near the woods.

Turn the page.

If you can make it there, you have a chance to lose your pursuers in the woods. Then you can make your way to the safe house.

As you reach the end of the tobacco field, two of the guards' dogs find you. They stare you down and growl, baring their teeth.

- To toss some of your food at the dogs to distract them, turn to page 26.

- To keep running, turn to page 29.

You decide to stick together and be quiet. You and your group remain huddled in the tobacco field. Everyone is still. You hear a guard ruffling through the tobacco plants. They're coming closer.

"I could've sworn that I saw movement over here. I'm not going to let them get away!" he mumbles.

Your group is panicked. Everyone looks to you to lead as the guards walk ever closer.

• To attack the guard, turn to page 27.
• To split up, turn to page 34.

You quickly pull out some bread and dried meat from your bag and toss it near the dogs. The dogs stop chasing you and begin to fight over the food on the ground.

That was close! you think, as you run away.

After another minute, you've escaped from the tobacco fields and have begun to enter the woods. In the distance, you hear the guards and overseers scream. They've caught some of your companions.

Despair overcomes you, but you know that you cannot stop running. You promise yourself you'll come back for whoever you can once you've found freedom.

Turn to page 29.

Together, you jump the guard and pin him to the ground. You cover his mouth to stop him from yelling.

"Let's gag his mouth and tie him up!" you order to the group. "If those guards and overseers hear him, we're done for!"

Quickly, the guard is gagged and tied up, but the sounds of the scuffle give you away.

"Over there!" an overseer screams. "Get them before they escape!"

The guards and dogs make their way toward your group.

"We have to split up. Run to the woods. Now!" you yell.

Most of the group flees into the tobacco fields. Xavier decides to stay by your side. You both make it into the woods.

Turn the page.

As you and Xavier run through the woods, you can hear your pursuers close behind.

"They're on our tail," Xavier says. "They're going to catch us!"

You grab Xavier by the arm and pull him off the forested path.

"Let's hide in the brush," you say. "Hopefully, they won't find us there. And once they pass us, we'll make our way to the safe house that can take us to the Underground Railroad."

The two of you push deep into the brush of the forest and hide. "Stay quiet and do not move," you say.

Turn to page 43.

You run deep into the woods, finally stopping to catch your breath. The only sound you hear is the wind rustling the tree branches. Your bare, calloused feet are sore, and you are very tired. You dig into your bag and find some dried beans. You eat a handful of beans and close your bag, while making sure that you don't leave any food crumbs on the ground.

Suddenly, you hear the overseer, guards, and dogs in the distance. You can see a trace of light as they get closer. They're carrying torches! It's time to keep running.

As you follow a narrow path deeper into the woods, you come to a fork. Do you take the path to the east, or the path toward the west?

• To take the path on the east, turn to page 30.
• To take the path on the west, turn to page 36.

You quickly take the path to the east. As you run, the path becomes filled with thick tree roots and unruly bushes. Pushing through the bushes causes a lot of ruffling noises.

"Over here! He went this way!" one of the guards' screams. "I'll get 'em!"

You run faster through the brush. The branches rip your clothing and cut you. But you can't tend to your wounds until you are safe.

A guard is getting closer. As you push through the brush, you trip on a tree root and tumble to the ground!

"Oof!" The fall takes the breath out of you. As you start to get up, the guard is only a few steps away. You're strong. Perhaps you could fight him off. Or should you just keep on running?

- To confront the guard, go to the next page.
- To keep running, turn to page 32.

You're probably too close to outrun the guard. Before he can yell to the others that he's found you, you push him to the ground as hard as you can.

He's knocked out! You take his torch, but you know that if you use it, that will make yourself a target. You toss it as far as you can in order to throw off the searchers.

The flame from the torch sets some of the brush on fire. It spreads quickly. Soon, the fields are aflame, and smoke is filling the air. The fire gets the attention of the others who are chasing you. It's a welcome distraction. You continue running as fast as you can.

Turn the page.

As you go deeper into the woods, you are forced to cut through a marsh. The guard dogs can't smell you after you've been in the water, so you should be a little safer now.

You continue on until you reach another fork in the path. You don't hear any overseers, guards, or dogs.

You take a moment to rest and ponder what to do next. From your bag of supplies, you take some roots and herbs and mush them together into a paste that you rub on your cuts. Hopefully, this will keep them from getting infected and help with the pain. Finally, you stand and consider your options. Should you turn left or right?

- To go left, turn to page 40.
- To go right, turn to page 45.

Enslaved people escaping through a marsh

You have to split up. Somehow, you make your way out of the tobacco fields undetected. The woods aren't too far away, but you spot what could be a quicker way to get away. To your left, there's a wagon with horses attached. It must belong to the guards. You decide to take it to speed up your escape.

As you make your way to the wagon, you see some of your group coming toward it as well. The overseers, guards, and dogs are on your heels. You jump into the seat of the wagon while the others get in. With a yank on the horse's reigns, the wagon takes off, and into the woods you go!

The wagon is going too fast for your pursuers to keep up. So far, things are going well. But you've never driven a wagon before. None of you have.

"There's a sharp turn ahead!" Xavier yells. "Slow down!"

You try, but it's too late. The wagon hits a tree and rolls. You and Xavier are thrown from the seat. The others in the wagon do not survive the wreck.

As you slowly get up from the ground, you hear gunshots and see torches. The overseers and guards are coming for you.

- To run away, turn to page 38.
- To quietly hide in the woods, turn to page 43.

The path to the west is clear, and you run as fast as you can. Its winding turns confuse you, but the fear of being caught and punished or killed pushes you to go on.

You feel like the path should be leading deeper into the woods, but it's not. Hopefully, it's far enough to take a moment to catch your bearings and figure out where to go next. Looking around, you get a sinking feeling. No, it can't be!

Four enslaved men are ambushed while attempting to flee.

The path has taken you back to where you started. Guards and dogs suddenly surround you.

"Looks like somebody went the wrong way," one of guards says. "Take him away and put him in the shed! No food for the next seven days! Let his suffering be a lesson for anyone who dares try to escape!"

Your journey to freedom is over. Perhaps you'll be able to try for freedom again someday.

THE END

To follow another path, turn to page 12.
To learn more about life after the Underground Railroad, turn to page 101.

You help Xavier up to his feet. His ankle is wounded.

"I'm too hurt to run," Xavier whimpers. "You have to leave me, or we'll both be caught."

Tears form in your eyes. "I can't leave you behind."

"Everyone else died in the crash. At least one of us needs to survive. You must go without me!" Xavier begs.

As difficult as it is, you gently lay Xavier back down on the ground. You know that he's right, but it doesn't make it any easier. You start to run deep into the woods and do your best to not look back.

While running, you hear a loud bang! You feel a hot, burning sensation enter and pass through your right shoulder. You've been hit! You tumble to the ground in pain.

"I got 'em, I got 'em!" a guard screams.

You wince in pain on the ground. You feel sick and dizzy as you bleed from the shot. The overseer and the guards stand over you as they smirk.

"Take him back to the farm and keep him alive," the overseer says. "Tomorrow morning, we'll make an example of him in front of the rest."

A guard taunts you as he chains you up, "When they see you getting whipped tomorrow, no one will try to escape again!" the overseer says.

The guards tie you up and begin to drag you back to the farm. Your end will soon be near.

THE END

To follow another path, turn to page 12.
To learn more about life after the Underground Railroad, turn to page 101.

This path in the woods is very spacious. It might be a well-traveled road for wagons and horses. Maybe you shouldn't have gone this way. It's nighttime now, but if you're still on this path when the sun rises, you'll easily be seen. You start to run.

The path leads you to a river. You don't know how to swim, and you don't want to get your supplies wet. Should you turn around and go back to the other path?

You don't get a chance to decide because suddenly, someone grabs you! Before you can say anything, they cover your mouth!

"Quiet!" said the voice. It's coming from a small Black woman. "Did you escape from a plantation?"

You nod your head up and down to say yes. She releases her hand from your mouth as you turn to face her.

"Shhh," she says. "Did anyone follow you?"

"Yes," you reply, "But once I got through the marsh, they lost my trail."

"Are there any others with you?" she asks.

"Yes, but we split up. I think some of them were caught." You pause and look curiously at this woman, before asking, "Who are you?"

The woman smiles. "They call me Moses. My real name is Harriet. I'm going to get you to safety. Down the river, there's a boat waiting to take you to a safe house. From there, we can get you to Philadelphia. I was leading a group of people to the boat when I heard you running in the woods.

Turn the page.

You let out a sigh of relief. You're closer to freedom than you've ever been. Harriet's confidence makes you feel safe and protected.

THE END

To follow another path, turn to page 12.
To learn more about life after the Underground Railroad, turn to page 101.

Harriet Tubman

In the brush, you and Xavier hear the guards running along the path in the woods. Both of you remain silent. You can see the light of their torches as they pass by. The fear of being caught overwhelms you.

Moments later, the guards are gone. You turn to Xavier and whisper, "Let's stay here a while just in case they double back. After that, we'll make our way back on the trail."

Xavier nods in agreement. "I think I hurt my ankle," he says.

Hours later, you continue your journey to freedom. You help Xavier walk on his weak ankle.

Suddenly, you're confronted by someone in the shadows. They have a gun pointed at you. You and Xavier raise your hands in defeat.

As the person emerges from the shadow, you both see that the shadow is a Black man, but he's wearing a freedman's clothes.

"My name is Andrew. I am an abolitionist. I also serve as a stationmaster."

"What's a stationmaster?" You ask. "Are you going to turn us in?"

"No," says Andrew. "I help Harriet Tubman and the Underground Railroad. Quickly, come with me and I'll get you to a wagon that will take you on a safe route to freedom before dawn."

You and Xavier follow Andrew, relieved. The journey to freedom and a new life is now closer than ever.

THE END

To follow another path, turn to page 12.
To learn more about life after the Underground Railroad, turn to page 101.

You decided to turn right. Everything seems fine until you round the bend and see your greatest fear. The overseers and guards have found you! You turn and run, but they chase you. Even giving it your all, you realize you're not fast enough. You know that you're going to be caught, so you stop running. Perhaps they'll be merciful if you give yourself up.

You turn around to surrender. But before the overseer can lay a hand on you, a group of armed men come out from the woods!

"Drop your weapons!" one of the men demands. Shocked, the overseer and guards surrender.

"Take their weapons, tie them up, and gag them," the leader of the group instructs the others. Then he looks to you. "Are you okay?"

"I am now. Who are you?"

Turn the page.

Abolitionists take on guards seeking to capture escaped enslaved people.

"We're abolitionists. Every night we patrol this area and keep a lookout for escaped enslaved people. By tomorrow morning, you'll be safe. For now, we have a medic that can tend to any injuries you have. Let's get you out of here."

THE END

To follow another path, turn to page 12.
To learn more about life after the Underground Railroad, turn to page 101.

CHAPTER 3

A CRATE ESCAPE

You live in Baltimore, Maryland. You are an enslaved laborer for a wheat mill that grinds grains for shipment across the country. It is a physical job. If you and the other enslaved laborers don't meet your daily goals, you won't receive any food or water. You may even be sent to death.

Tonight, you lie in your quarters, counting down to the moment you'll make your move. You can't live like this anymore. It's time for you to risk it all.

Turn the page.

A while ago, your cabinmate told you the story of the enslaved man who shipped himself to a free state in a crate. He started a whole new life. You're not sure if the story was true or not. But it sounds like a good idea to you. You're tired of being forced into a life that you did not ask for. You want to be free.

An enslaved man named Henry Brown shipped himself to freedom in 1856.

One day, while loading some flour on a wagon for deliveries, the driver asks you to talk to him for a moment.

"I'm sorry sir, but if I don't finish loading your wagon fast enough, I'll be punished."

The driver, a white man, responds. "It's all right. I told your supervisor that I needed to talk to you. It's about how you're loading the wagon. Come take a look with me. You're not balancing the weight correctly. It can damage the wheels," he says.

You were taught by your supervisor how to properly load a wagon, and all the bags are evenly laid out. You're baffled, but you don't want any trouble. You follow him and hop inside the wagon.

The man quickly whispers. "We don't have much time. Your sister sent me a message to give to you."

Turn the page.

"Maya!" you exclaim. "How do know my sister? Is she safe?"

"Lower your voice!" the man says. "Yes. She is safe. She's free now and works to free others. We have folks at the post office who will ship you to Harrisburg, Pennsylvania. Your sister is there. The third and sixth delivery wagons that come through the mill tomorrow will be the best way for you to escape. You'll need to find a way to sneak onto the wagon. They will have a crate you can hide in."

"What happens when I get in the crate?" you ask.

"Those wagons go into town for drop-offs and home deliveries. Plenty of enslaved folks run errands, so you can get out and blend in with them. Head to the post office and tell the postmaster that you have a special shipment that needs to be secured."

You nod your head in agreement.

"Be ready tomorrow," he says.

As you leave the wagon, the driver signals the horse to get moving.

Your heart thumps in anticipation. You can't believe you'll actually be free soon—and see your sister. But which wagon should you take? If you take the third wagon, you'll get into town when more enslaved people are running errands. You'll be able to blend in more easily. But you might also be missed at the mill the earlier you leave. Maybe you should take the sixth wagon.

- To sneak onto the third delivery wagon tomorrow, turn to page 54.
- To sneak onto the sixth delivery wagon, turn to page 56.

The next day, you're filling bags of grain. You've been keeping an eye on the wagons coming in and out of the mill. The first two wagons came in, filled up on supplies, and went on their way. An hour later, the third wagon arrives. You worked out a deal with your cabinmate the night before to help you. In turn, you promise to find a way to help him escape at a later date.

The driver of the wagon steps down and takes the mill boss outside for a talk. You recognize this as a distraction. The wagon is now unguarded. You look at your cabinmate and give him the signal.

"My heart!" Tyler screams as he collapses to the ground. "It's pounding so fast! I—I can't breathe!"

The floor supervisor and the other enslaved laborers surround Tyler. You quietly step away while no one is looking and hop into the back of the wagon. You quickly look for a crate large enough to fit into. The apple barrel would be big enough, but it's half full. You doubt that's where you're meant to hide.

Suddenly, you hear the driver and your boss making their way back inside the building before you've found a crate to fit in!

- To keep looking for a better crate to hide in, turn to page 58.

- To squeeze into the apple barrel, turn to page 60.

You convinced your supervisor to let you work the later shift so you can escape on the sixth wagon. When the wagon arrives, a few enslaved laborers begin to load it. The driver chats up the mill boss to distract him. Meanwhile, some of the enslaved laborers ask the supervisors to help with a damaged grinder. It's the chance you need to get into the wagon.

But when you look, there are no crates! There's nothing large enough to hide you. Before the boss and wagon driver come back around, you look underneath the wagon and notice a compartment. You think you can hold on in there.

Moments later, the wagon leaves the mill and heads to town. The ride is extremely bumpy. You try your best to hold on and not fall out of the bottom of the wagon. An hour into the ride, you're exhausted from trying to hold yourself in the compartment.

Inside a grist mill grinding wheel

- To continue trying to hold on, turn to page 62.

- To tumble out of the wagon and take your chances on your own, turn to page 67.

You quietly open the crates. One is filled with clothing, sheets, and yarn. It's a big soft place to hide. You get in and quietly close the lid.

"What's going on in the mill?" says the driver, as he hops into his driver's seat.

"I don't know, but I'm about to find out," says the mill boss, as the wagon drives away.

The wagon makes its way to town. "We're about halfway there. I'll let you know when everything is safe," the driver says.

You rest inside the crate. It's a hot day. You're sweating buckets on the clothing and sheets, but it's still better than being in that wheat mill. And soon, you'll see your sister again.

Suddenly, you hear gunshots! Voices yell. You hear the thundering hooves of horses chasing the wagon.

"Stop and give us your valuables!" says a gruff voice. You can tell from the sound of horse hooves that there is more than one rider. Should you stay in the crate and hope you're not discovered, or should you hop out the back and hope to make a run for it?

- To stay in the crate, turn to page 69.
- To escape from the crate and try to make it on your own, turn to page 70.

You quickly squeeze into the apple barrel. It's a tight fit, but you make it work. You cover yourself with apples to play it safe as the wagon drives away.

Finally, the wagon comes to a stop. You've made it to the town. The driver leans toward the cargo and says, "Don't come out until I say."

The driver leaves, and you hear someone on horseback pull up beside the wagon.

"I need to talk to you for a moment," a gruff voice says. He's talking to the driver. "A mill a couple of towns away has a missing worker. Do you know anything about it?"

You try not to panic. You're so close to seeing your sister again. You can't get caught.

"I haven't seen anyone," the driver replies. "I inspected this wagon before leaving the mill, and all that's in there are goods for the general store."

The man grumbles. "Well, let's go talk to your boss. There's a nice reward for this guy. Maybe he's seen something."

The driver and bounty hunter walk away. You know that it's not safe, so you stay in the barrel. Then you hear other footsteps approach.

"Get the stuff out of the wagon that goes to the general store immediately," says a woman. "The store is about to close, and it's late. Hurry up."

A bunch of workers unload the items from the wagon and put them in the general store, including you in the barrel of apples. You remain quiet and wait for everyone to leave. Minutes later, all is quiet. Is it safe now?

- To wait a while longer before you escape, turn to page 72.
- To exit the barrel and try to find the post office, turn to page 74.

You keep holding on, but then it starts to rain. Mud and water splash you. You can't hold on much longer. You're about to fall out from underneath the wagon.

Suddenly, there's a CRACKKKK! The wagon slides to a stop as the back left wheel breaks off. The wagon collapses. You're not sure how to feel. On the one hand, the wagon is broken. On the other, at least you're not worried about falling out anymore.

The wagon driver hops off his seat onto the muddy road. He looks under the wagon, but he doesn't notice you in the compartment.

"Hmmmm . . . I think I can repair this," he says. "But I can't do it alone."

You can't tell if he's talking to you or to himself. Does he know you're here? Is this even the right wagon?

You couldn't find the crate you were told to hide in. Maybe you missed the sixth wagon and this is the seventh. Should you reveal yourself and offer to help or stay hidden?

Goods loaded into an old delivery wagon

- To help the wagon driver, turn to page 64.
- To continue to hide, turn to page 66.

You tumble out of the compartment and land face first into the mud.

SPLAT!

The driver is surprised to see you. "I didn't think anyone was aboard! My people told me that someone would be hiding in the wagon, but with all the bags of grain, I didn't think that it would be possible."

"I had to improvise," you say as the rain continues to fall. "Is there anything that I can do to help us get this wagon moving again?"

The driver nods. "I think so. You wait there, and I'll get my tools from the wagon."

Just then, you hear running horses. It's three bounty hunters! These men track down enslaved people who try to escape.

"That must be the one who escaped from the mill! Get 'em!" you hear.

Within moments, you are surrounded. You're going to be taken back to the mill. You may even be executed in front of the other enslaved people. But you're not sorry you tried to escape. You gave it your best shot.

THE END

To follow another path, turn to page 12.
To learn more about life after the Underground Railroad, turn to page 101.

Staying in the compartment shelters you from the rain. The driver is eventually picked up by someone on horseback.

You hope you picked the right wagon and that someone knows you're here. You had thought this was the sixth one, but now you doubt it. You don't know how far away you are from the town, so you don't want to risk going out on your own.

Suddenly, you hear a creaking noise. The wagon starts to shake and rumble. The weight of all the wet grain in the wagon begins to buckle the axles. You try to get out from the compartment in time, but the axles break. You are crushed by the weight of the wagon. Your last thought is of your sister.

THE END

To follow another path, turn to page 12.
To learn more about life after the Underground Railroad, turn to page 101.

You tumble from the bottom of the wagon and roll around the dirt road as the wagon continues to go on without you. You take a very hard bump which knocks you unconscious. You end up tumbling into the brush.

Hours later, you awaken. You're soaking wet. It must have rained. You struggle to remember what happened as you rub your head. You probably should've tried to hang on to the wagon. At least it's nighttime, so no one will spot you as you flee.

You get out of the brush. It's very quiet. The road is clear as you begin to walk.

You go on for hours before realizing you're lost. You have no idea where to go for help. You don't know who is friendly and who will turn you in. For days, you avoid bounty hunters who were hired by the mill to find you and bring you back.

Turn the page.

After a week, you're dehydrated, and you haven't eaten much. You have no idea where you are. All you can do is hope to stumble into someone who will help you. You may die of starvation before that happens, but at least you'll die free.

THE END

To follow another path, turn to page 12.
To learn more about life after the Underground Railroad, turn to page 101.

Without a word, the driver commands the horses to run. He's going to try to outrun them!

You panic. How can a wagon full of supplies outrun men on horseback?

But your horses are fast! The robbers don't catch up.

Suddenly, the driver attempts to take a sharp turn at full speed. The wagon overturns! It tumbles off the road and crashes down the steep side of a rocky hill, and splashes into the river.

You've made a valiant attempt at freedom, but neither of you survive. At least you died a free man.

THE END

To follow another path, turn to page 12.
To learn more about life after the Underground Railroad, turn to page 101.

You quickly scramble out of the crate and run from the wagon, but it's no use. The robbers catch you easily. They tie up you and the wagon driver.

"Looks like this driver was carrying a stowaway!" said the leader of the gang. "What should we do with them?"

One of robbers speaks up. "Get rid of them both and take what we want!"

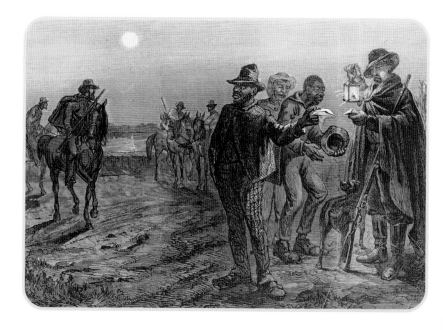

"I don't think so," says the leader. "We can get rid of the driver, but I bet somebody's looking for this boy. Might even get a hefty reward for bringing him back."

Your heart sinks. You would have preferred death to being sent back to the mill. You grimly await your fate as their prisoner. You can only imagine what the mill owner will do to you when you return.

THE END

To follow another path, turn to page 12.
To learn more about life after the Underground Railroad, turn to page 101.

You wait a while longer, until you're sure no one is around. You're climbing out of the barrel when a door opens. You crouch back inside.

"I always forget my hat," says a man's voice. You guess it's the store owner.

"There it is, sir," replies a younger man's voice.

The door closes. That was close! The coast is finally clear, so you climb out of the barrel. From the store window, you see that it's evening, and the streets are empty. The post office is across the street. There is still a light on inside. You quickly run to the post office and tap on the door. It opens, and an old lady stands before you.

"I'm sorry," she says, "But we're closed for the night. You'll have to wait until tomorrow to ship anything."

You begin to worry, but you suddenly recall what the driver told you to say.

"I have a special shipment that needs to be secured," you say. "Please, help me."

The old lady smiles, knowingly. "I was starting to wonder if you survived the wagon ride after that bounty hunter came to town. Come in. You'll sleep here tonight. In the morning, we'll put you in a crate going to Harrisburg, Pennsylvania. Let's get you a hot meal and a change of clothes."

You've never known such kindness. It seems too good to be true.

But it is true! The next day, you squeeze into another crate with a satchel of food. After a long journey, someone finally opens your crate. It's your sister!

THE END

To follow another path, turn to page 12.
To learn more about life after the Underground Railroad, turn to page 101.

All is quiet in the general store, so you climb out of the barrel. As a few of the apples from the barrel hit the floor, you hear a voice.

"Hello? Who's in there?"

You thought everyone was gone! You panic as you scramble out of the barrel and fall to the floor.

THUMP!

The store owner and his family run over to you.

"What were you doing in this barrel?" the owner asked, pulling out a gun.

The owner's wife chimes in, "Don't even think about running."

She turns to her son and says, "Go get the sheriff. Tell him we have a runaway! We're going to get a big reward for this!"

Your chance for freedom is no more. In a few moments the sheriff will arrive, and you'll be sent back to the mill. And you will be severely punished for trying to escape.

THE END

To follow another path, turn to page 12.
To learn more about life after the Underground Railroad, turn to page 101.

CHAPTER 4

RISKING IT ON THE UNDERGROUND RAILROAD

You escaped from enslavement three years ago. From then on, you decided to join the abolition movement and work on the Underground Railroad. You help to free enslaved people.

Your current mission takes you to Louisville, Kentucky. You and your group have snuck into the state on the river. Your boat carries freight and mining supplies, but it's just a cover for helping people escape enslavement.

Turn the page.

Late at night, you creep onto a large farm that serves as a forced labor camp. You tell one of the enslaved workers that in two nights, you are going to set fire to the fields to cause a distraction.

"When the owners and overseers run to put out the fire, make your way to the orchard," you tell the man. "We'll be waiting for you. We'll take you on our boat to Ohio. Tell whoever wants freedom that we'll help them."

The man nods his head. "Me and my people will be ready," he says.

The night has finally come. You and a group of armed abolitionists wait in the orchard, as one of your team members sets the crops on fire.

It's not long before you hear cries of, "Fire! Fire!" The farm owner and his guards race to put out the flames.

Meanwhile, a group of enslaved people run toward the orchard. You stand there and wave them toward you.

"Follow our men. They'll take you to a secret tunnel that leads to our boat. I'll be right behind you. Go-go-go!"

You turn to follow them when you hear a scream for help.

The flames have spread faster than you'd expected. A young, enslaved girl screams from the fields, the flames all around her.

- To follow the others and continue the mission, turn to page 80.
- To go save the young girl, turn to page 81.

The flames are too high to save her. Your heart breaks for the girl as you follow the others.

Suddenly, a guard hops out of the brush. "Your people started this fire, and you're gonna pay for it. None of you will make it out of here alive!"

The two of you fight and drop to the ground. The guard is very strong. He puts you in a choke hold that takes your breath away.

- To try to roll the guard over to escape, turn to page 83.
- To try to break guard's choke hold with your hands, turn to page 97.

You can't just leave her there. You yell to your team, "Get to the boat. If I'm not there in five minutes, go on without me!"

You run through the fiery fields. The flames rise as the girl screams. You follow her cries to find her. The heat is nearly unbearable, but you can't let this girl perish.

Turn the page.

Moments later, you find her. "Don't worry child, we're getting out of here. What's your name?"

"Nadia," she says with tears in her eyes.

"Cover your face, Nadia," you tell her.

You pick her up and run out of the flames. As you reach the edge of the field, you see the guards in the orchard. *Can't go that way*, you think.

You know there's a safe house nearby, but you'd have to go by road. That would leave you exposed. Perhaps you should run through the woods.

- To find the safe house, turn to page 87.
- To run away through the woods, turn to page 90.

You try rolling over so that you're on top of the guard, but he really has you pinned. You're about to pass out.

Suddenly, you hear a *BLAP!* The guard loses his grip on you and collapses to the ground. You catch your breath and rise to see a young Black girl with singe-marked clothing, holding a large stick.

"Are you okay?" she asks.

"I am now, thanks to you," you reply, gratefully. Shame washes over you as you realize she was the girl caught in the flaming fields.

"I ran through the fire and saw the guard on you. Luckily, there was a shovel nearby," she says, holding it up. "My name is Nadia."

Turn the page.

You take her hand. "Nadia, I owe you my life. Now let's hurry and catch up with the others. We can't miss the boat!"

You run to the secret underground tunnel. A man near the entrance of the tunnel raises his pistol at you.

"Stop right there!" he demands. He is a custodian. These people assist in escapes by guarding safe routes and safe houses in slave states. Often, secret passwords are used, so he asks, "What is the drinking gourd?"

You know the right answer. "The drinking gourd is the Big Dipper and the North Star," you reply.

The custodian smiles. "Hurry! The tunnel will take you to the river. The rest of the group came through a few minutes ago, and they won't wait much longer!"

You and Nadia crawl through the tunnel. As you exit, you see the boat about to take off.

"Wait! Don't leave us!" you scream, as you and Nadia chase the boat down. Two of the members of the team have their arms extended out at the end of the boat.

People fleeing enslavement by boat at night

Turn the page.

"Hurry! We'll pull you in!" they yell.

The guards from the farm and bounty hunters have found you! They fire at the boat. You and Nadia finally reach the boat, but she is having a hard time getting on, even as the others pull her up. You could give her a push, but then there might not be time for you to get in.

- To let the others help Nadia and pull yourself in, turn to page 94.
- To help get Nadia on the boat, turn to page 95.

You pull Nadia's hand and run in the direction of the safe house. It is a few miles away, in the hills of Louisville. The guards won't go there. They're scared of the "hill folk" as they call them.

"I don't feel so good," says Nadia, coughing.

You know that she inhaled a lot of smoke, and her head is very hot, while the rest of her body is ice cold. She is not well. "The safe house will have everything we need to get you to feeling better."

"What's a safe house?" she asks as you pick her up.

"It's a place where bad folks won't find you. You'll be protected. We'll be there in a bit, I promise."

Turn the page.

It seems like you've been carrying Nadia forever. You need a moment to catch your breath. You gently place her on the ground and take a deep breath. "We're almost there, just a few more miles—OW!"

A searing pain shoots through your leg. You've been bitten by a snake. It's too dark to tell what kind of snake it is. You quickly pull some salve from your pouch and rub some of it on the bite. If it's poisonous, the salve will help.

"Are you okay?" asks Nadia.

You take a deep breath and exhale. "I'll be fine. I just forgot to look for snakes out here. We'd best keep moving."

You pick Nadia back up and carry her to the hills. You are starting to get warm. You might be running a fever from the snake bite. Your vision becomes blurry. As you get closer to the safe house, an armed custodian comes out to greet you.

"What's the code word?" he says, with his weapon drawn at you.

"Gospel Train," you gasp, "Please, help her. She's inhaled smoke and has a fever."

As you hand Nadia to the custodian, you collapse to the ground.

"Please sir, help him! He was bitten by a snake!" Nadia cries.

"Don't you worry, little girl," says the custodian, as more people come out to help you. They pick you up and take you inside the safe house. "We're going to make sure both of you will be all right. Soon, we'll get you to a place where you'll be free."

THE END

To follow another path, turn to page 12.
To learn more about life after the Underground Railroad, turn to page 101.

The path in the woods is more protected than the road. And it runs parallel with the river. Hopefully, you can make it to the boat.

The little girl is whimpering while you carry her. You slow down for a moment. You don't want the girl's cries to give you away. "Listen, I know you're hurting, but you have to be very quiet, or bad people might find us."

It's then that you notice the burn marks on her. She's in a lot of pain. You lay her down and pull bandages and salve from your pouch and wrap her burn marks and wounds. "Is that better?"

"Yes, sir. Thank you, sir," she responds.

"You're welcome. I'm going to pick you back up, and we're going to get you to the boat. Try not to make any noise, okay?"

Turn the page.

People fleeing enslavement at night

As you leave the woods, you see the glimmer of the river and your boat in the distance.

"We're almost to the boat. We have a doctor who will check your burns, and we'll get you something to eat so you can feel better, okay?"

"Okay, sir," she says.

Finally, you reach the boat.

"Thank goodness you made it!" says one of your crew members. "We were about to leave!"

You're thankful to have made it in time. You gently hand the girl over to a member of your crew.

"Take her to the doctor," you say. "She has severe burns and needs treatment. Let's get out of here before trouble shows up!"

As the boat begins its getaway, you breathe a sigh of relief. Because of you, a group of formerly enslaved people will soon be free to start a new life.

THE END

To follow another path, turn to page 12.
To learn more about life after the Underground Railroad, turn to page 101.

People escaping enslavement by boat

You selfishly pull yourself up into the boat. In doing so, you get hit by a hail of gunfire. Meanwhile, the others have managed to get Nadia on the boat safely. The boat goes full speed down the river as it makes its escape.

You fall to the ground.

"He's been shot!" Nadia screams. "Somebody, help him!"

A doctor comes out to tend to your wounds, but it is too late. Perhaps you got what you deserved. Twice, you put your own safety ahead of that of a young woman. You die with your shame.

THE END

To follow another path, turn to page 12.
To learn more about life after the Underground Railroad, turn to page 101.

You give Nadia a push, and it gives the folks on the boat enough reach to save her! She's out of harm's way. But it's not looking good for you.

You're beginning to tire out, and now the guards are shooting at you. You leap to hang onto a boat rail, but you're starting to lose your grip!

Suddenly, a rope appears!

"Grab onto the rope! We'll pull you up!" one of the crewmen yells.

Moments later, you're safely on the boat. Soon, your enemies are far in the distance and out of reach.

Nadia runs up and gives you a big hug and starts to cough. You yell for the doctor, "She inhaled a lot of smoke and has some burns. Please, help her!"

Turn the page.

"Thank you for saving me," Nadia says, as the doctor takes her away. You smile, but you can't help but think you should have done more. You vow that you will.

In a few days, you'll be on another mission to free more enslaved people, and you won't rest until all of your people are free.

THE END

To follow another path, turn to page 12.
To learn more about life after the Underground Railroad, turn to page 101.

Using all your strength, you peel the guard's arm off of your neck. You try to hurry and catch your breath, but the guard is relentless!

He comes at you again! You're still trying to get your breath and strength back as the guard is overpowering you. This may be the end.

Suddenly, some of the men of your team attack the guard. They have come back to help you!

"We waited so long, I knew you must be in trouble," one of the men says. "So, some of us came back to help."

"Thank you," you say, honestly grateful. "But you shouldn't have risked missing the boat because of me."

Another man replies. "The boat is secure, and we can still make it. Let's go!"

Turn the page.

You, your team, and the newly freed folks make your way through the tunnel and back to the boat. After being saved yourself, you regret not helping the girl in the fire. You are thrilled when you reach the tunnel and find that she was able to get out on her own. You and your team have saved a lot of lives today. Soon, they will be able to live freely.

THE END

To follow another path, turn to page 12.
To learn more about life after the Underground Railroad, turn to page 101.

CHAPTER 5

AFTER THE UNDERGROUND RAILROAD

From the early 1800s until the American Civil War (1861–1865), the Underground Railroad helped get about 100,000 enslaved people to freedom. Many of these people came from the mid-Atlantic states such as Virginia, Maryland, and Kentucky. They bordered free states. These states had abolished slavery. Very few enslaved people escaped from the deep south.

In 1863, President Abraham Lincoln issued the Emancipation Proclamation. It liberated enslaved people in Confederate states. The Confederacy battled the northern states over slavery during the Civil War (1861–1865). After the Union won the Civil War, the 13th Amendment to the Constitution of the United States put an end to slavery in America.

Black Americans reading the Emancipation Proclamation

Even though Black people were now free, the battle for equality was far from over. Between 1865 and 1877, Black people made great strides in politics and business. This time period was called Reconstruction. But many white people were not happy about it. They did not want Black people to have equal rights.

Soon, Jim Crow laws were passed in the southern states and throughout America to a lesser degree. These laws kept Black people from being allowed to vote, be elected to office, or live in white neighborhoods. This segregation was also used to keep Black people from accessing white schools, public pools, water fountains, theaters, hospitals, parks, and many other places. Marriage between Black people and white people was outlawed. Many places had signs in their towns letting Black people know that they were not welcome there.

In 1948, President Harry Truman made an executive order to desegregate the military. This made a small dent in the wall of Jim Crow. In 1954, the Supreme Court ruled that schools could no longer be segregated. They said that Black children deserved the same education as white children.

Civil Rights leaders such as Martin Luther King Jr., John Lewis, Roy Wilkins, Aileen Hernandez, Diane Nash, and others led the fight for freedom and equality. In 1964, the Civil Rights Act was established. The following year, the Voting Rights Act passed. It allowed Black people and other people of color equal voting rights.

When the Fair Housing Act of 1968 passed, it marked the end of all Jim Crow laws. However, America still struggles with race relations, injustice, inequity, and inequality to this day.

Five generations of Black Americans

Stories of the Underground Railroad are an important part of American history. They remind us of the struggles and pain that Black people have endured in the past. And it inspires us to continue the fight for equality and equity for all.

Timeline

Early 1800s
Quaker abolitionist Isaac Hopper starts helping enslaved fugitives.

1830s
Abolitionist David Ruggles begins to work with Isaac Hopper, helping at least 600 people escape enslavement.

1841
Formerly enslaved man Josiah Henson creates the Dawn Settlement. The institute helps formerly enslaved people learn job skills and how to live independently.

1844
The language of the Underground Railroad, using code words such as "station masters" and "conductor" begins to be used.

1849
Henry "Box" Brown escapes enslavement by shipping himself in a wooden box.

1849
Harriet Tubman escapes enslavement and goes on to become the most well-known conductor of the Underground Railroad.

1850

Congress creates and passes the Fugitive Slave Act, which wrongly forces formerly enslaved people to be returned to their owners.

1861

The Civil War begins.

1863

Black soldiers began to fight for the Union against the Confederacy.

1865

The Union wins the Civl War. The 13th Amendment frees Black Americans from enslavement.

1868

The 14th Amendment grants citizenship to Black people.

Other Paths to Explore

1. Imagine you are an enslaved person who wants to escape, but your loved ones are too afraid to try. Would you leave without them? What might you do to try to change their minds?

2. Working on the Underground Railroad came with many risks. What kind of training might these people have needed? Do you think you would have been brave enough to risk your life to help people who you don't even know reach freedom? Why or why not?

3. Enslaved people gave plantation owners free labor. Can you think of any other reasons why plantation owners may not want enslaved people to be free?

Bibliography

Black Past: The Underground Railroad (1820-1861)
blackpast.org/african-american-history/underground-railroad-1820-1861/

Bordewich, Fergus M. *Bound for Canaan: The Underground Railroad and the War for the Soul of America*. New York: Amistad, 2005.

Craft, William and Ellen. *Running a Thousand Miles for Freedom—The Escape of William and Ellen Craft from Slavery*. Athens, GA: University of Georgia Press, 1999.

Executive Order 9981, Desegregating the Military
nps.gov/articles/000/executive-order-9981.htm

History.com: Underground Railroad
history.com/topics/black-history/underground-railroad

Larson, Kate Clifford. *Bound For the Promised Land: Harriet Tubman: Portrait of an American Hero*. NY: Ballantine, 2004.

National Archives: 13th Amendment to the U.S. Constitution: Abolition of Slavery (1865)
archives.gov/milestone-documents/13th-amendment

Still, William. *The Underground Railroad: Authentic Narratives and First-Hand Accounts*. Minneola, NY: Dover Publications, 2007.

Glossary

abolitionist (ab-uh-LI-shuhn-ist)—a person who worked to end slavery

amendment (uh-MEND-muhnt)—a change made to a law or a legal document

axle (AK-suhl)—a bar in the center of a wheel around which a wheel turns

dehydrated (dee-HY-dray-tuhd)—not having enough water

lash (LASH)—a mark made by being whipped

overseer (OH-vur-see-uhr)—a person in charge of watching and punishing enslaved people

salve (SAV)—medicine or lotion that relieves pain and helps heal wounds or burns

shackles (SHAK-uhlz)—pair of metal cuffs for the wrist or ankle of a prisoner

unconscious (uhn-KON-shuhss)—not awake; not able to see, feel, or think

Read More

Enz, Tammy. *Science on the Underground Railroad*. North Mankato, Minnesota: Capstone Press, 2023.

Tyner, Artika R. *The Untold Story of John P. Parker: Underground Railroad Conductor*. North Mankato, Minnesota: Capstone Press, an imprint of Capstone, 2024.

Wesgate, Kathryn. *Uncovering Depots of the Underground Railroad*. New York: Enslow Publishing, 2023.

Internet Sites

History.com: Underground Railroad
history.com/topics/black-history/underground-railroad

The Underground Railroad
education.nationalgeographic.org/resource/underground-railroad

Underground Railroad
kids.britannica.com/kids/article/Underground-Railroad/353882

JOIN OTHER HISTORICAL ADVENTURES WITH MORE
YOU CHOOSE SEEKING HISTORY!

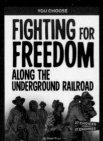

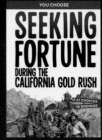

About the Author

Shawn Pryor is the creator and co-author of the graphic novel mystery series Cash and Carrie, co-creator and author of the 2019 GLYPH-nominated football/drama series Force, and author of *Kentucky Kaiju* and *Jake Maddox: Diamond Double Play*. In his free time, he enjoys reading, cooking, listening to streaming music playlists, and talking about why Zack from the Mighty Morphin Power Rangers is the greatest superhero of all time.